CHOOSING LIFE

ECOLOGICAL CIVILIZATION AS THE WORLD'S BEST HOPE

JAY MCDANIEL AND JOHN B. COBB, JR.

I0191617

Topical Line Drives
Volume 41

Energion Publications
Gonzalez, Florida
2020

ISBN: 978-1-63199-565-1
eISBN: 978-1-63199-573-6

Energion Publications
P. O. Box 841
Gonzalez, FL 32560

energion.com
pubs@energion.com

TABLE OF CONTENTS

INTRODUCTION

WHAT'S CHRISTIAN ABOUT THIS BOOK?

Though we write this book for people of all faiths and none, we write this book as Christians and yet, as you read, you may sometimes wonder where the Christianity is. Where is Jesus? Where is God?

For us there is a healing spirit at work in the universe and in the world that was revealed uniquely, but not exclusively, in the healing ministry, death, and resurrection of Jesus. This healing spirit is God. We want to live our lives in service to the healing spirit as revealed in Jesus. We want to share in his journey, his experience, and his faith, and thus to be channels of love. We align ourselves with, and are grateful for, communities of people who seek the same, otherwise called the church. Yes, we write as Christians.

JESUS

Like all Christians we are moved by three aspects of Jesus' life: his healing ministry, death, and resurrection of Jesus. From his healing ministry we see the healing spirit at work in the lives of individuals who were transformed in mind, body, and spirit and also in communities that were transformed. His aim was to encourage and empower communities of people who would care for one another and live their lives guided by love. These communities embody what he called the basilea tou theou: a state of affairs when the will of God is done on earth as it is in heaven. From his death and the fact that he responded to being killed, not by hatred but by forgiveness and understanding, we realize that there is a side of God that is empathic and vulnerable; a side which receives and absorbs the sins and sufferings of the world in a non-retaliatory and loving way, refusing to hate even enemies. In his death as well as in his life, he shows us a God who is, in the words of the philosopher Whitehead, a "fellow sufferer who understands." And from his resurrection we see that the healing spirit is at work in the world through the provision of new and hopeful possibilities for life, even amid the most devastating of circumstances. We see that God is a source of comfort and new life - in this life and in whatever continuing journey there may be after death. Inspired by these and so many other dimensions of Jesus' life and teachings, we want to walk in his footsteps and share in his faith. This book, then, has these kinds of commitments at its core.

GOD

You may also sense some "process theology" in what we say; we are indeed process theologians who understand God in terms of ten key ideas. We can state them plainly here:

- God's unchanging aim is for beauty, understood as rich-ness of experience.
- God seeks salvation for each and all: universal richness of experience.
- God is in the world through fresh possibilities or 'initial aims.'
- We feel God's feeling and share in God's desires. God is within us and within all living beings, even as more than them all.
- God is both eternal and everlasting: non-temporal and infinitely temporal.
- God is nowhere and everywhere: non-spatial and om-ni-spatial.
- God is lovingly affected by the world: a "fellow sufferer who understands."
- God saves the world through tenderness.
- God is many as well as one, in the sense that the universe is part of God's own life.
- God recycles love.

To these ten we can add two more.

- God is not in complete control of the world; God acts through love, not domination.
- The future is open, even for God. God knows what is possible in the future, but not what is not yet actual.

3

These ideas concerning God are important to us, including the last one. We think that the future is open, that it can unfold in ways profoundly disastrous for the world God so loves, and that it can unfold in ways that are life-enhancing. We believe that God's hope is that we choose life. And we believe that choice requires fresh thinking: imaginative, analytical, political, economic, poetic. You'll find elements of all in this book.

CHAPTER TWO

CHOOSING LIFE

In the Bible there is a famous saying from Deuteronomy where God says to the people of Israel, and by implication to us all, "Now choose Life." We are reminded of a note found on a napkin in a local diner, written by a student from the liberal arts college down the road. In her way she was trying to choose life, too.

> *Dear Life,*
>
> *You are so beautiful and yet I know you're in sad shape. In my own life there are some problems. I won't go into the details but I know you understand. I'm part of life, too. And then there are the big problems: global climate change, disappearing species, cruelty to animals, economic disparities, ethnic nationalisms, violence and war, the meaninglessness of consumer culture. Part of me wants to hide from it all and seek a private happiness. But this part never quite wins out. Might I carry a little hope for you and, in my own way, make a constructive difference in the world. Hoping to hear from you.*
>
> *Or, to be more honest, I know you're hoping to hear from me.*
>
> *Deborah*

This book is for the Deborahs of the world. We are among them and perhaps you are, too. Like Deborah you may feel distressed and depressed about the future of the world. We feel this way, too. Nevertheless, you may carry a hidden hope for life that you can't quite escape. It is a hope for the flourishing of life and its well-being. You hope for the well-being of your own life and the lives of your friends and family. You hope for the well-being of other people whom you don't know, and who may live in distant parts of the world or close by. You hope for the well-being of the

5

more than human world: the animals and plants, hills and rivers, trees and stars. No matter how dark the world can be and seem, there lies within us the flickering of a dream to be happy with others, such that our happiness and theirs are intertwined. It is a hope for what Martin Luther King, Jr. called beloved community. We call it the compassionate community.

This hope has a very personal side. As Deborah put it: "I am a part of life, too." And it simultaneously rooted in a desire to live in truly compassionate communities that are creative, kind, participatory, inclusive, diverse, inclusive, humane to animals, good for the earth, and spiritually satisfying, with no one left behind.

We believe that the building of these communities in local settings is part of what Thomas Berry calls the great work of our time. It is "great" because it is important and necessary; it is "great" because it is creative and satisfying; it is "great" because it is more than us but beckons us from within the depths of our spiritual genes. What beckons us? It is something difficult to name but natural to feel. Call it "Life" or "God" or "Love" or "Beauty." Let there be many names for it and also, when silence is best, no name at all. Named or unnamed, it is something that is on the side of life and that needs our cooperation for its fulfillment. As Deborah says, it hopes to hear from us.

Deborah might think that, because she is a college student, she cannot yet enter into the great work, but this is not true. Education at its best is for the whole person, not simply for succeeding in the marketplace or developing research skills that will never be used. Education in the arts and sciences can play a role in the building of these communities. On the one hand compassionate communities have objective qualities that can be understood with help from the social and natural sciences. They consist of physical realities – streets and buildings, living spaces and commercial spaces, rivers and forests — that can be seen with the eyes, touched with the hands, and measured. But these communities also partake of forms of relatedness, qualities of heart and mind, that are best communicated through the arts and humanities: attention, compassion, connection, curiosity, devotion, gratitude, hospitality, imagination, wonder, imagination, playfulness, silence, and a sense of mystery,

6

for example. In this book we speak of these forms of relatedness as spirituality. A compassionate community needs the objective and the subjective, the scientific and the humanistic, the practical and the spiritual, gathered into the unity of a general cultural ethos that is enjoyed by all, especially those who might otherwise be left out. Communities of this sort are the building blocks of what we call Ecological Civilization.

Ecological Civilization is our name for a kind of civilization that is grounded in respect and care for the community of life, with special care for the vulnerable. We do not use the word ecological to name environmental problems alone. We use it:

- to evoke a sense of integral ecology that hears and re-spond to two cries simultaneously: the cry of the earth and the cry of the poor;
- to evoke an intuition that we are small but included in a creative web of mutual becoming filled with countless forms of life, all of which have their value and beauty, and
- to suggest that there is something like life or vibrant energy within the whole of the physical world, which means, in the words of the philosopher Whitehead, that "nature is alive."

We hope that you can hear these three meanings in our use of the word ecology: integral ecology, mutual becoming, and the aliveness of nature. An Ecological Civilization is a civilization in which the three ideas just named are part of the cultural atmosphere of the society as a whole, and in which they inform the politics, economics, urban design, rural life, infrastructure, and feeling tone of the society as a whole.

Ecological Civilization can be embodied in many different settings and partake of many different cultural flavors: African, East Asian, South Asian, North American, South American, European, and more. It is a needed alternative to the kind of civilization we know throughout the world today. Some call it "modern" civili-zation; it might also be called "un-ecological" or, perhaps better, "dying civilization."

Truth be told, most of us live in a dying civilization grounded in the opposite of the three ideas named above. It is spread by the worst aspects of global capitalism and the shallowness of consumer culture, which is the 'religion' of capitalism. It is premised on the ideas:

- that human problems and environmental problems can be understood and solved separately, and that some human beings don't really matter at all.
- that humans are skin-encapsulated individuals who are isolated from one another and who are apart from, not a part of, the larger web of life.
- that the more-than-human world – the hills and rivers, the trees and stars – is but a lifeless machine consisting of materials to be used and abused for human consumption.

Part of the great work of our time – especially among philosophers and artists, scientists and theologians — is to critique these three ideas and to help all of us enter into an outlook on life that affirms integral ecology, mutual becoming, and the aliveness of nature.

But of course we are not all philosophers, artists, or theologians. The great work can be undertaken in many other ways, and we naturally undertake the work from different walks of life. Waitresses and clerks, teenagers and the senior citizens, Baptists and Buddhists — our strength lies in our diversity. Our shared hope is that communities of this kind can emerge all over the world, each with its own cultural flavor. And it is that the world itself might grow into a community of communities of communities in which we respond to Life's calling. Deborah's hope is our own. We write this book to fan the fires of hope.

CHAPTER THREE

FIVE FOUNDATIONS FOR AN ECOLOGICAL CIVILIZATION

In order to undertake the great work of building compassionate communities, we must be honest about the need for fundamental change. Truth be told, our un-ecological civilization hastens to self-destruction both locally and globally. The deep changes needed to stop or slow this wholesale rush are not even on the table for discussion. We are taught by consumer society that our primary calling in life is to pursue fame, fortune, and power.

In the opening chapter we identified three ideas important to Ecological Civilization: integral ecology, mutual becoming, and the aliveness of nature. In this chapter we spell this out further by identifying the basic assumptions of our dying civilization and indicating the alternative that could give life to a new one. Any success we may have in promoting these positive assumptions will also moderate the disasters that lie ahead.

FROM INDIVIDUALISM TO COMMUNITY

One strength of modern European civilization was its emphasis on the individual. In most societies, including the Medieval one against which the Enlightenment reacted, the potential ability of all to become creative and self-determining individuals was encouraged only among the few. The Enlightenment gave vitality to the idea that every individual counted and had rights as well as duties. Unfortunately, it also built separate individuality into its metaphysical assumptions. This led to reflections about morality that ignored both the importance of belonging to something larger than oneself and the deep sense of mutuality that builds up healthy communities. The resultant individualistic ethical reflections, institutionalized in economic thought and practice, came to dominate political and social thought.

Ayn Rand's libertarianism has become the authority for all too many leaders in American society. The rich and powerful no longer feel responsibility for the poor and weak. Ruthless exploitation is increasingly accepted as the norm. Selfish behavior has always been a problem, but it could be countered by appeals to concern for others and for the common good.

But in today's society, these appeals are regarded as sentimental. It is thought that realistic and tough-minded people should pay no attention. Checks on Individualism are rapidly eroding just at a time when the survival of civilization depends on deep commitment to the common good.

Moral understanding reflects metaphysics. If we want a society in which the sense of belonging is strong, people are concerned for one another, and there is strong commitment to the common good, we need a metaphysics that shows that we are in fact part of larger societies and have no existence apart from our relations to others. Our individual good is dependent on the common good.

From Sense-Bound Empiricism to Radical Empiricism

Associated with the view of each entity as a separate individual is the view that the individual's knowledge of the external world is gained entirely through the sense organs. We call this empiricism. Given the fundamental metaphysical assumptions of modern European thought, it appears self-evident to many. Its adoption helped to overcome many superstitions and gave rigor to scientific development. When we appeal only to what we touch and see, we can usually agree. Scientific consensus is possible. Enormous progress has occurred.

However, the civilizational cost has been enormous. The Enlightenment originally took for granted that there is also a world of thought and subjective experience that is just as important as the "natural" one studied. Freeing science from distortions arising from subjective beliefs played, on the whole, a positive role.

Sadly, over the course of time modernity gave privileged status to the "objective" world and the methods by which it was studied. The tendency has been to absorb some of what was once the province of humanistic investigation into the "hard" sciences and dismiss what cannot be fitted into this expansion of science. The world of values was relegated to the margins or excluded altogether. The ideal for research, and then for education generally, was to be value free. That meant that there could be no judgment as to what should be studied other than what someone would pay for. The purpose of gaining an education was to prepare oneself for a better paying job.

But civilization is based on judgments of importance and value. For example, a civilization must be concerned about the world it provides for its children. Today, many speak of the value of sustainability, but it still plays a very marginal role in our intellectual, political, and educational institutions. When we downplay other values, the default value is money. Supported by this value, the rich and powerful orient themselves to their own economic flourishing and inform us that we cannot afford "sustainability."

The remedy is not to reject empiricism but to enlarge it. William James called for "radical empiricism." When we change our metaphysics so as to recognize how our very being, our basic experience, is constituted by relations with others that are not constrained by sense data, we will be ready to understand that much else in our experience is just as useful in the quest for wisdom as what modernity has allowed us to consider. A healthy civilization can be built on radical empiricism.

FROM WE/THEY THINKING TO WORLD LOYALTY

While the thought-life of modernity has been shaped by extreme individualism, the actual life has been formed much more on the basis of the we/they divide. We are in fact social beings. For hundreds of thousands of years our ancestors lived in small groups that could survive only by strong social cohesion. Changing social structures partially shifted the understanding of "we" to larger groupings. Gender also plays a role universally. Later religion came to be an important factor in identifying the "we." For modern Europeans, nations came to dominate the self-identification of most people.

Of course, the situation is more complex. Local communities, institutions or professions can be the basis of this we/they divide. Marxism focused on class, with the primary division between capitalists and workers. Today, the most important divide may be between the super-rich and the rest of us.

11

The Enlightenment also supported this we/they division between human beings and the rest of the world. One could appeal to its principles to develop a universalist humanism or a religion of humanity. Not long ago something that was called "scientific humanism" played a significant role in the intellectual community. However, this ideal had little effect when it became fully separate from the traditional faith that gave rise to it. The Enlightenment teachings gave no reason to be concerned about strangers or people in other parts of the world. Modern empires had no hesitation in exploiting the conquered. The deeper we/they feelings set the conquerors over against the conquered and provided little sense of their togetherness as a "we."

That any we/they ordering of human concerns is inherently destructive is obvious. As technology draws humanity more and more together, we increasingly need to identify ourselves in a more inclusive way. Whitehead speaks of the need for world loyalty. A new civilization must order itself and its teachings so as to hold the inevitable we-they distinctions in check, always emphasizing the larger whole to which both we and they belong.

FROM ANTHROPOCENTRISM TO BIOPHILIA

There have been anthropocentric tendencies in most civilizations. But none has been as systematic in this regard as that of the modern West. The dualism of Descartes juxtaposes the human mind to everything else – even the human body. Animals are part of the world that is turned over to science for objective study. They are not supposed to have any subjectivity. Although Westerners, for the most part, do not really believe that animals have no subjectivity, our treatment of animals today, as we raise them for food, reflects this dominant theoretical position. Even those who call for avoiding the extinction of animal species typically provide only anthropocentric arguments.

Earlier we indicated the importance of reaffirming the marginal Enlightenment view of humanity as the crucial "we." This certainly cuts in the right direction on many issues, but it does not touch this one. As long as serious and influential thought remains completely anthropocentric, the likelihood of real restraint in wiping out other creatures is slight. This is true even when the consequences are obviously deleterious to us — as in extreme overfishing of the oceans and damaging of its physical capacity to sustain marine life.

We need to expand the ideal of benevolence towards all human beings to biophilia. Children have biophilic tendencies. These can be encouraged, whereas they are now taught to think of them as merely sentimental. A biophilic civilization can be a sustainable one.

Our own judgment is that biophilia needs further support. We need to understand life as a force present everywhere including in us. It is not only what makes us alive, but also what heals many of our sicknesses and injuries. Of course, doctors do much to free it to do its work. It is the same force that leads to more complex forms of life and finally to love and thought. It is a force with which we can seek to align ourselves. Whereas biophilia relates us well to particular living things, it is also important to devote ourselves to the service of this life force. As we said earlier, call it Life, God, Beauty, or Love. In the final chapter we'll say a word about what it means to call it God.

From conventional morality to counter-cultural morality

Although in intellectual discourse, morality as a whole has lost its force, society depends on a measure of conventional behavior. Also, few parents really believe that right and wrong are completely meaningless ideas. Indeed, most children are brought up legalistically. There are things they are taught they must do, and others, they are taught they must avoid. In many instances these do's and don'ts are associated with religion. Because sex is an area in which most parents feel the need to restrict their children's behavior, many of these moral rules deal with that.

Many of the rules are good in the sense of promoting smooth functioning of the family and the larger society. But some create guilt of a useless and even damaging sort. The experience of discovering the arbitrariness of some of the rules of conduct learned in childhood is a major factor in anti-religious feeling as well as the widespread belief in the relativity of moral teaching.

The role of morality in Western civilization has markedly declined. What remains is largely conventional, and conventional morality, among other things, supports the *status quo*, whatever that is. Today the *status quo* is a society committed to its own destruction.

Especially in our present society we need a countercultural morality. That requires taking very seriously our responsibility to live rightly and a strong sense that "right" is very different from "wrong." But it requires an equally strong skepticism about rules that specify do's and don'ts. It calls for a radically non-legalistic morality, one that places the well-being of the whole created order above any rules and regulations.

REDEFINING OUR CALLING

As we redefine our collective calling, there is a place for the individual, for local communities, for science, for conventional morality, for religion, for joy. But our very capacities for becoming whole people are enriched by questioning the five assumptions named above, and as we explore alternatives, we can help bring new life to a dying civilization.

The need is to move beyond preoccupations with *my* calling to *our* calling as creatures among creatures on a small planet. Part of the problem of individualism in the modern world lies in the assumption that callings are always individualized. They can be collective, too. We may live in Asia, Africa, Latin America, Europe, North America, or Oceania. We may be young or old or in-between. We begin where we can begin, with the only day we have today: *today*. With the courage to challenge modern ways of thinking, there is hope. In the next chapter we offer five practical steps for realizing this hope.

Chapter Four

Practical Steps Toward an Ecological Civilization

We live on a small planet orbiting a medium-sized star in a middle-sized galaxy. Even if we destroy all life on our planet, Earth will continue in its orbit. We need not and cannot save the planet. We can simply be awed by the fact that, for a moment in cosmic history, we are small but included in a larger multi-galactic journey.

But in our time cosmic awe is not enough. It has never been enough. There is a need for biophilia, a more intimate appreciation of life on earth, including human life. The beauty and diversity of life on our planet needs saving; and we too need saving. In this chapter we offer some practical steps.

EDUCATION SHOULD BE FOR WISDOM

The modern worldview has shaped education and transmits itself through the education it has shaped. Because that worldview is misleading and has let modern society astray, contemporary forms of education do more harm than good. That does not mean that they do no good. They do a great deal of good. But overall they contribute much more to human destruction of the Earth's capacity to support life, and thus to human self-destruction, than to saving us from this fate.

The problem is not with the earliest years of education. In kindergarten, teachers focus on the children and their healthy development. But all too rapidly attention is redirected toward subject matter and skills needed to support and advance the economy. Given the ordering of society to the economy, and the nature of the economy to which it is ordered, there is no question but that fitting into the economy is essential for the well-being of workers. And in these circumstances it seems rational to prepare children for this. The problem is that this kind of education only prepares children for participation in an economy that is dying, a death that will bring with it enormous suffering. Those equipped only to fit into a destructive economy will cling to that economy as long as possible, however apparent its destructiveness becomes.

Higher education is much more problematic. The norm for this level of education has come to be the research university. It is understood that successful research isolates one range of data and develops methods to study in that field. The result is called an academic "discipline." The ideal is to organize all knowledge into disciplines each of which adds to the information available to human beings. To accomplish this, the disciplines must be value-free. One topic is as appropriate for research as any other.

To some extent research will reflect personal interests of researchers. However, as the low hanging fruit is picked, research tends to become more expensive. As a result, most of it is governed by the availability of funding. Since money is available chiefly for medical, corporate, and military purposes, most research is in these fields. Since the research university is value-free, evaluating research projects in terms of who is benefited and how is irrelevant

The vast majority of research is strictly determined by the current status of thought in the discipline in which it occurs. Established methods are employed. What cannot be studied by these methods does not concern the researcher. In most disciplines there are debates about methods and theories, and this assures researchers of the intellectual substance of their work. But there is little study of the history of the discipline and little reflection about the basic assumptions in the context of which the debates take place.

The research university has vastly increased the amount of information that is available to humanity. But it has given little or no guidance as to how this information should be used. It offers little or no criticism of the assumptions of the modern world that have led to the extreme overshoot that now dooms it to collapse. It engages in little or no research about the changes in society and the economy needed to attain sustainability.

If we ask where in the university one can gain help in understanding what is going on in the world today, the answer is everywhere. But of course the information gathered in many independent lines of research has no coherence and provides little guidance. In any case the university does not judge that saving civilization from collapse is any more important than solving some problem for the military. That global warming is speeding up is an interesting fact, but it is no more important than information about football scores.

Some professors ignore disciplinary boundaries and think coherently about the global crisis, but they are not rewarded by the university for doing so. The research university is typically composed of departments for numerous academic disciplines supplemented by professional schools. Whereas in the earlier years of education, pupils are prepared for the workforce, the university prepares people not only to be researchers and professors but also to be managers, doctors, teachers, lawyers, engineers, and so forth. In each case specialized work in some disciplines provides important information, but the practical concern of the profession affects the professional school as it does not affect the disciplines.

In contrast to all of this, an Ecological Civilization calls for an education-oriented to wisdom. Of course, every society needs to prepare its youth to participate in the society including its economy. And of course, we need institutions where research can be conducted on many fronts and some members of the next generation can learn to do this research well. But we also need, with truly desperate urgency, institutions that seek wisdom and encourage youth to learn how to gain it.

The quest for wisdom is continuous with the concern for personal development in the early years. Wisdom is an important characteristic of the mature person. In past centuries higher education was more directed to personal development including wisdom. The liberal arts were thought to be beneficial in these respects. Even today there are liberal arts colleges that encourage a kind of thinking that does not fit into the academic disciplines. Sadly, they have difficulty finding teachers who have not been socialized into disciplinary research as the ideal.

Advocates of Ecological Civilization will struggle to maintain a serious role for the liberal arts in higher education. Nevertheless, a return to a classical understanding of the special role of the liberal arts will not fulfill the calling of higher education today. The liberal arts were developed at a time when there was no apparent threat to the biosphere on a global basis. They are anthropocentric, whereas we live in a time when the integration of human life and the rest of nature is of primary importance. They tend to encourage individualism, albeit one that accepts social responsibility. They tend to be elitist, separating those who want to make good use of leisure from those who only want to be entertained.

Wisdom is expressed in the judgment of importance. The refusal of the research university to make judgments of this kind is an abrogation of responsibility for the fate of the Earth. A Whiteheadian judges that not only should the university make judgments as an institution, but it should also shape its curriculum as directed by critical reflection about what is important. Further, encouraging students to participate in this critical reflection and to relate it to their own decisions about research projects and careers should shape the life of the university as a whole.

This in no way means the abandonment of special foci. The world needs physicists and engineers, teachers of children and economists. But physicists and engineers should decide on their research and projects out of concern for the flourishing of the biosphere with particular attention to the human species. Teachers of children will need to reflect about how to introduce them to the realities of their time without overburdening them with anxieties before they are ready to cope with them. Economists should stop tinkering with their ideas about how to make the economy grow and ask what kind of an economy the world can afford and how to move quickly in that direction. In every field, basic assumptions should be constantly articulated and reconsidered.

We have discussed what it would mean to make wisdom the most fundamental goal of education only at the level of higher education. But this form of higher education should not be an abrupt break with earlier education. Reflection about the condition of the biosphere and the prospect for humanity in this context is important for younger adolescents as well. They, too, are capable of wisdom, if society encourages them in that direction.

18

THE ECONOMY SHOULD BE DIRECTED TO THE FLOURISHING OF THE BIOSPHERE

The most important revolution in history is the industrial one. Prior to it, there had been many important changes in the way of life of masses of people, but the capacity of people to produce goods and services in an agricultural economy had not varied greatly over time. In almost all societies the masses of people lived on the land at a subsistence level, while a few gained wealth by siphoning off the excess over that needed for the subsistence of the farmers. This surplus supported life in towns and even cities, where a middle class of artisans, merchants, and professionals developed alongside an urban proletariat. A few lived in great luxury. In general, the limited availability of food for the poor played a primary role in preventing rapid population increase.

What was discovered in the eighteenth century was that the same number of workers could produce a great deal more. The early focus was on the production of clothing and furniture and household goods and tools and machines. It turned out that by organizing workers in assembly lines and supporting them with energy from coal, production per hour of work could be vastly increased. There could be abundance of goods that had formerly been scarce and their price could be greatly reduced. What had formerly been luxuries for the rich could now be made available to the masses.

From the beginning there was a price to pay. The satisfaction artisans felt in their work was denied to assembly-line workers. Factories brought with them new kinds of pollution. The aim at profit for the investors in a factory led to exploitation of labor that was in some ways more vicious than the exploitation of peasants in the countryside. Industrial cities were typically filled with slums. Unemployment became a problem rarely experienced in agricultural societies. The landed nobility saw that its power was passing into the hands of industrial capitalists. *Noblesse oblige* gave way to a single-minded quest for profit. Not everyone was pleased by the changes effected by industrialization, but there was little prospect of turning back the clock.

Over time the industrial model was applied more and more widely. Eventually, agriculture was also industrialized, and features of the industrial method were applied to merchandising as well. Increasing productivity, defined as production per hour of labor became the norm everywhere.

The industrial economy required larger markets. There were economies of scale; so that one huge factory could often underprice several smaller ones. But to sell its product it needed more customers. This affected international relations as industrial powers sought markets all over the world.

Factories often needed natural resources not plentiful locally. Hence nations whose policies were driven by economic concerns were also interested in securing supplies of such resources. There was another great advance of empire building. There was also a drive, especially after World War II, to make of the whole globe a single market, so that goods could be produced wherever conditions were most favorable and sold wherever they were in demand.

Modern economic theory beginning with Adam Smith grew up alongside industrialization. The economists explained the benefits of industrialization and sided with industrialists against those who wanted to curtail their freedom. They saw not only factory production but the whole of the economy as ideally geared to "growth" measured by total production of goods and services per capita. They were strong advocates of the move toward a global market.

Mainstream economists have based their study and theories on industrial society. Today the financial sector has come to dominate the productive one. It clearly dominates government as well. Its control of the money supply is a major source of its power. Economists have far less understanding of this phenomenon than of the industrial economy it supersedes. Markets controlled by banks are not free.

We might expect that economic theorists would be concerned with the ability of the environment to supply all the raw materials needed for a growing industry. However, they have largely dismissed this problem. They note that as a particular resource becomes scarce its price rises. This leads users to be more frugal and efficient with this resource and also to seek more plentiful, and therefore less expensive, substitutes. Such scarcity also leads inventors to find new ways of meeting the need that does not require the scarce item. Economists assure us that economic signals lead to developments that by-pass the problem of scarcity. They do not view resource scarcity as placing any limit on growth. Although there has been less discussion of pollution until very recently, economists try to subsume this under the same type of response. Those few who argue against unlimited growth of the human economy are viewed as outsiders to the community.

The idea of "overshoot and collapse" comes from zoology and has no role in mainstream economic thinking. Today, the acute problem of global warming calls for the application of this concept to human affairs. But thus far it has been excluded from economic theory. Economists remain cheerleaders for economic growth everywhere and under almost any circumstances. They have been deeply misled by the modern worldview in its most harmful form.

Fortunately, largely outside of academic departments and of the economics guild, others are developing an ecological economics that emphasizes the issue of scale. They note that the human economy is a subset of the natural economy and must remain a limited portion. As long as the natural economy is limited, the human economy must also be limited

Ecological economists redefine the goal of the economy. One important contribution to this task is the book, "The Economics of Happiness" by Mark Anielski. (New Society Publishers, 2007) We have found that the growth so prized by economists does not, in any regular way, make for the happiness of real people. To pursue growth when it does not contribute to the well being of people is quite mistaken. The task of economists is to find ways of organizing the economy that contribute most to human well-being. The Kingdom of Bhutan now measures its wellbeing in terms of Gross National Happiness.

A major shift that helps redefine the goal of economics is that from the individualism that underlies all mainstream economic theory to an appreciation for community. We now know that, beyond a very limited level, personal happiness is more a function of human relations than of the quantity of goods and services consumed. Unfortunately, modern thought has led economists astray. They have ignored human relations other than those of contract and exchange. Often the way of benefiting people is to improve the quality of the communities in which they live, but the application of modern economic thought has systematically destroyed communities.

Focusing on community does not mean rejecting economic growth. Many communities are improved by increasing the supply of fresh water, food, improved shelter, education, and medical care. However, forcing people to leave their communities in order to find employment rarely adds to human well-being.

Even "economics for happiness" does not go far enough in our time. As Anielski and the rulers of Bhutan fully understand, human happiness cannot be separated from the flourishing of the whole ecosystem. We need an economic theory directed to the regeneration of the global biosphere.

The move toward an ecological economy will require breaking the control of financial institutions over both industry and government. The key to this is recovering for community, at whatever level, the control over the money supply. The present global economy is collapsing. Rather than trying to stave off this collapse, we can use the occasion to build local economies that serve their communities well. This will be a profound reversal of long-term trends. It may include state and municipal banks and local currencies that free the community from subservience to the international banks. Local economies can encourage frugality and sustainability instead of growth. They need not look to growth to solve the problems of the poor. Instead, the local community will accept responsibility for providing work for all who want it and for meeting the essential needs also of those who cannot work. We may exchange the "high" standard of living measured by the surfeit of goods for a secure place in a healthy human community in a healthy ecological context.

AGRICULTURE SHOULD REGENERATE THE SOIL

Apart from human experience the normal situation is one in which the seasonal cycles gradually build up the soil. It becomes more fertile and thereby accelerates its own growth. When human beings lived by hunting and gathering, this increase of soil continued. The change came with the rise of agricultural societies. These found that they could produce a great deal more of the desired plant nearby if they cultivated the soil and planted only that one crop in a particular plot. Farming developed in many contexts and many styles. Some were far more sustainable than others, but all reversed the trend from building up topsoil to using it up, however slowly.

Some ancient civilizations ended when the land they farmed, for one reason or another, lost its capacity to support them. This should have been a warning to others of the applicability to agriculture of the "overshoot and collapse" model. But in general new lands were found to cultivate, and some of the old ones seemed to be inexhaustibly rich. In any case there seemed to be no alternative. Agriculture had produced the food that allowed population to grow. To sustain that population, the damaging cultivation of crops must continue. If that meant moving people to new land, so be it. As long as the global population was small in relation to the amount of cultivable land, the problem seemed minor.

For thousands of years the basic agricultural situation did not greatly change. But in the nineteenth, and especially the twentieth, centuries industrial methods were applied to agriculture. Family farms gave way to agribusiness. Agricultural science studied the chemical needs of plants and the ways that weeds and noxious insects could be killed. Fertilizers and poisons came into more extensive use. The condition of the soil became less important since the needed nutrients could be supplied artificially. Monocultures became more extensive.

Genetic changes of plants were designed to adapt them to the new chemical regime. The wide variety of species of wheat or corn was replaced by the one species able to deal with these chemicals. Huge machines replaced both human and animal labor. Large areas of the countryside were depopulated.

The main gain from all of this was "productivity" as measured by produce divided by hours of human labor. Economic theorists celebrated this gain as releasing farm-workers to do other jobs. Ecologists fretted that soils were losing their natural fertility and eroding more rapidly, while agriculture was becoming more dependent on irrigation and petroleum products. They also worried about the loss of genetic diversity and about the effects of artificial varieties on natural ones, on the environment in general, and on the health of those who consumed them.

From the perspective of an Ecological Civilization, ecologists are right to worry. Farming has kept the human involvement with nature very intimate for thousands of years. Despite human manipulation, agriculture was primarily a process of working with nature. The application to agriculture of modern economic theories developed in relation to industry makes the whole process highly precarious. It also makes it dependent on resources that are becoming scarcer and scarcer: fresh water and oil.

As we look to the future, we see what is needed as evolving from traditional family and peasant farming, hoping to recover the land now used for agribusiness in a more traditional way. We certainly affirm the organic form of production to which the Cubans were forced by the lack of oil. But we recognize that even organic farming is exploitative of the soil, and as the soil diminishes, the future looks dim. The task is to stop the exploitation and find ways to follow the natural processes that build soil instead.

There have been many positive developments alongside the negative ones involved in agribusiness. No-till agriculture shows that the plowing that exposes the land to the wind can be avoided. Certain combinations of plants can greatly decrease the loss to insects. Irrigation can be accomplished with much less water by systems that use it only where directly needed.

We who are rich have become accustomed to having almost any food at any time of year. This is a luxury afforded to us by the global economy. As we prepare for its collapse, we will think of eating locally-grown food instead. That will reduce variety, but it can also have advantages. Fresh food organically grown has its own excellence.

A movement in this direction is already well advanced. There are thousands of farmers markets all over the country, encouraging this change in eating habits as well as the farmers who are growing the food. There is also a widespread movement of urban agricul-

24

ture. It may be most fully developed in Detroit where there are many vacant lots and houses and many people unemployed. In the residential area of Los Angeles County in which I live there are efforts to make unused land available to unemployed Immigrants from Mexico who know how to use it. Thus far these movements of local food production are marginal to the food industry as a whole. But their growth will make a great difference with respect to who and how many can survive the collapse of the global system.

Where land is limited and the need for food is great, extremely intensive food production will be needed. Examples of this already exist. A family of six in Pasadena feeds itself on food from its own quarter-acre lot. It also sells some specialty items to nearby restaurants to earn cash. Another development may be even more important in the long run. Although intensive labor methods can do much to end the erosion of the soil, we can also learn quite new methods of farming. Wes Jackson at the Land Institute in Salina, Kansas, has noted that the vast American prairie developed its rich topsoil during millennia in which it was covered by a polyculture of perennials. When European farmers came, they replaced this with a monoculture of annuals. The loss of soil began.

We have generally assumed that the grains that are so essential to our food supply must necessarily be annuals. Jackson notes that there are perennial forms of corn and wheat, but that their yield is far less than that of the annuals we have cultivated. However, he does not believe that perennials are inherently less productive of the seeds that humanity needs. He has set out on a fifty-year experiment in developing highly productive perennial grains, and he has made great progress. This is the kind of research to which our universities should be devoted instead of the study of how to make tomatoes that are better able to withstand shipment over long distances.

Another change in eating habits will enable more people to survive the collapse. Most of us are addicted to eating meat. We eat far more than most people through human history. And we eat far more than we need for health or is even healthy for us. In many instances ten times as many calories of grain are fed to the animals than are present in the flesh that we eat. Dramatic reduction of meat-eating will enable more grains to be available for more people.

When we approach the question of meat-eating with this question alone in mind, the goal will be to end the eating of grain-fed animals, but not complete vegetarianism. There is land that is suited to pasture but not to farming, and producing meat may be its best and most sustainable use. Also, the most fully integrated use of a small farm often includes animals. They can eat what would otherwise be wasted and produce natural fertilizer for use on plants. The consumption of surplus animals is an efficient contribution to our food supply.

An ecological vision leads many, however, to become vegetarian on other grounds. The animals we kill have their own intrinsic value. Killing them may not be as destructive of value as killing other human beings, but it is the same kind of evil. Such killing, a Whiteheadian may well believe, should be reduced as much as possible. Avoidance of eating meat can be our contribution.

There is yet another relevant argument. From the perspective we embrace, all inflicted suffering is inherently evil. Whatever may be theoretically possible, the reality is that today much, probably most, of the meat that is served to us has been raised in ways that are cruel to the animals. Their suffering is often life-long rather than only a matter of the moment of death. Our consumption of meat supports an industry that is brutally indifferent to animal suffering.

COMFORTABLE HABITAT SHOULD MAKE MINIMAL DEMANDS FOR RESOURCES

In the days of cheap land, cheap transportation, and cheap utilities we built millions of large, poorly-insulated homes on large lots in suburbia. We used a lot of lumber in home construction, sacrificing our forests in the process. Our individualism led to nuclear families replacing extended ones and to separating ourselves even from our neighbors. We typically found our communities with like-minded people elsewhere than in our neighborhoods. Our homes were for ourselves and our children, and we expected others to respect our privacy as we respected theirs.

We are now entering a world in which land will be needed to produce food locally, and transportation and utilities will be expensive. We will need to increase tree cover rather than further decimate our forests.

Obviously, much of our task will be improving what we have. We can greatly reduce our use of utilities by insulation. We can generate much of our own energy with solar panels. We can also work to develop cooperative relations with neighbors to save on the number of separate car trips that are needed and perhaps buy some kinds of equipment for the neighborhood. And we can use some of our land to produce food.

This is important and for some time it may be the best contribution we can make to staving off collapse. However, in this section I want to focus on the kind of construction that should, over time, replace what we now have. Fortunately, there has already been a lot of experimentation with buildings that provide comfortable habitat without requiring the further decimation of forests or extensive use of utilities for heating or cooling.

MOST MANUFACTURING SHOULD BE LOCAL

It is fairly obvious that when humanity finally decides to end its suicidal burning of fossil fuels, producing goods in one place and shipping them around the world will end. This is one part of the collapse of the current civilization that is readily predictable. Of course, one possibility is that our addiction to fossil energy will persist so strongly that we will turn to fracking to keep the global civilization going at whatever cost to human life and the biosphere. If so, we will probably destroy the capacity of the planet to support any human life at all. If we turn to nuclear energy on an ever larger scale, the threat to survival will change its nature but not be removed. This paper is presupposing that the human race will stop short of suicide.

If we do, the question of how we can live in a sustainable way confronts us. Which of the good things we now receive from our global civilization will we be able to continue to enjoy? We have considered thus far only food and shelter. But there is a vast world of manufactured products that we would like to retain. Can we do so?

The answer is that no one knows just what will be possible. We can say, however, that a shift from manufacturing for global distribution to more local production is a given. The ideal would be a rather gradual transition. As transportation becomes more expensive, heavy and bulky items will be increasingly produced nearer their destination. If common sense leads to greater restrictions on burning fossil fuels, this tendency will be accelerated and even smaller and lighter goods will be produced more locally. A transition of this type would be far less disruptive of our lives and societies than was the globalization of production that has caused so many of our problems. It will, of course, be part of the localization of the economy discussed earlier.

However, transportation of goods is not the only problem. Industrial production has been based on fossil fuels. A great deal of thought is now directed to other sources of energy. The most promising are wind and direct solar forms. Small scale local production can be based on wind and solar energy far better than the huge centralized productive facilities now dominating the scene.

The most difficult problem is that many of the natural resources needed for manufacturing are not locally available in most places. To whatever extent their shipment is ended, the goods made from them cannot be produced. This will call for a great deal of ingenuity. As long as this is available, many needs can be met with locally available materials.

Consider, for example, clothing. Cotton and wool are major raw materials for much of this. But there are many parts of the world where neither is available. Fortunately, we have long since learned that clothing can be made from fibers of many sorts. Stores would not carry the vast variety of clothing we now take for granted. But the real need for clothing could be met almost everywhere in the world.

One obvious problem with local production is that it is impractical for many of the things we take for granted. The automobile is an example. A city, even of a million people, could hardly produce automobiles efficiently if its market was limited to that city. Certainly the city could not support several competing companies.

The ideal response is that cities should be so constructed as to make automobiles unnecessary, and we may indeed hope that they will move in this direction. We can imagine that private cars can be eliminated without disaster, difficult as that will be. But public transportation requires vehicles the local production of which in many places would be even more impractical. It is difficult to imagine a painless transition in transportation from the collapsing global society to a sustainable local one.

Two directions of change in regard to urban transportation may take place. One is the abandonment of public transportation as well as private cars. This would force city dwellers to organize life in relatively self-sufficient neighborhoods within which bicycles would be the major means of transportation. The other is for megacities to develop the capacity to produce what they need for public transportation. Powering this system of transportation, as well as the factories that manufacture the vehicles, without fossil fuels is a separate problem.

Another broad change can be imagined and encouraged. We have become accustomed to cheap, disposable, mass-produced goods. Most of us Americans have far more goods than we need. Our problem is to store them or clear out our closets to make room for new ones. This flood of goods replaced a situation in which most of the things people really needed were produced by hand and were durable. Today handiwork is more of a hobby than a primary occupation, but a shift back in this direction would be a welcome one. If handiwork were prized and its products could be profitably sold, unemployment would cease to be a major problem. We would use fewer resources and own fewer goods, but what we would have would bring us greater satisfaction and its production would be a creative rather than a routine act.

Finally, we may hope that the vast world of electronic communication can survive the collapse of the global economy. In the new order, the travel we have so enjoyed would become a rare luxury. But this would not need to disconnect us with the rest of the world. We could be citizens of the world in touch electronically with like-minded people elsewhere. When successful adaptations to the new global situation are developed in one place they can quickly be shared with people around the world. People in obscure villages could listen to the lectures of the world's most advanced thinkers. The best knowledge in medicine could be made universally accessible. We need not consider localization of production the enemy of wide horizons of thought and action.

EVERY COMMUNITY SHOULD BE A PART OF A COMMUNITY OF COMMUNITIES.

The collapse of the global economy and all the institutions connected with it will force people to make do with local resources. If they approach this task with the same mindset that has created the unsustainable global economy and the overshoot of the earth's resources, the future for humanity is very bleak indeed. This book is written to encourage an alternative. Humanity will have the opportunity to construct local communities.

A community is not automatically generated by people living in close proximity. Most suburban neighborhoods today are not communities. A community gives identity to its inhabitants. When nation-states arose, they intended to be communities. Their citizens identified themselves in large part by their nationality. They expected the nation as a whole to take some responsibility for the welfare of all its citizens and were willing to make some contribution to enabling the nation to do so.

The organization of Europe in terms of nation-states was part of the rise of modernity. It weakened local communities and communities based on religious identity for the sake of strengthening the national community. Nevertheless, much of the economy remained local, and local community remained strong. The industrial revolution greatly weakened local economies and increased mobility within the nation. Local communities lost much of their importance and often ceased to function as communities. This whole process was strengthened by the individualism that was encouraged by Enlightenment thinking.

This individualism has now been turned against the national community as well. The economic elite no longer identify themselves particularly as American. If they belong to any community, it is a transnational one of wealth and power.

It is no longer self-evident to many Americans that they should be prepared to contribute to meeting the needs of all Americans. That idea, rooted in the very meaning of community, is dismissed as "socialist" by an increasing, and increasingly influential, segment of the population. They believe the national government should give them freedom and support their interests. It should protect them from interference by other people. But it should not expect any contribution from them for other purposes.

The now developing global crisis can lead to fresh reflection that will make people aware of the importance of community. If it does so, this will express itself most clearly at the local level. Confronted by acute shared problems, we may hope that people will agree that they need to work together for their solution and to build a new life. The preceding sections have sketched, in the most hopeful way, what will be possible.

The major problem with communities is that they are in danger of defining themselves over against other communities. Individuals who identify themselves strongly with one community may perceive others as actual or potential threats. The we/they understanding of the world easily arises, with "they" understood negatively. A world composed of local communities all of which face scarcities of important types is threatened by conflict that can easily become violent. That sort of world is unsustainable.

Hence the goal must be not only to have strong, healthy local communities, but to have also communities of communities. We can see something like this in the world of sports. Consider the high school teams of small towns. The citizens of those towns feel a strong sense of identification with their teams and root for them vociferously. But the teams that compose a particular league also gain some of their identity from their participation in that league and want it to be strong and healthy. Also when wider concerns are in view, those who root for their teams show their concern for the other towns that support the other teams. The rivalry among the teams is contained in a context of sportsmanship, and the teams learn the importance of respecting their rivals.

31

Healthy local communities will have as part of their basic self-understanding a respect and appreciation for other communities and their citizens. If one community suffers a natural disaster, its neighbors will come to its aid. It is healthy to have competition and rivalry, but this is not healthy unless it is contained within a wider context of respect and cooperation.

Local communities will have their relatively self-sufficient economies, but there will be economic issues that require cooperation with their neighbors. Those that *only* compete will not survive, and they will destroy others along with themselves. Healthy communities will participate in communities of communities. Although each will have considerable autonomy, any effort to be completely independent will misfire. Communities of communities will also need the authority to make decisions. And the same is true of communities of communities of communities. Even in a world in which the focus is on the local, there will be need for some governance at the global level as well.

A political structure of this sort will be sustainable only if we overcome individualistic ways of thinking. In the modern world this individualism has expressed itself not only in the erosion of community at the local and national levels but in the idea that at one level or another there must be "sovereignty." That need springs from "substance" thinking. Process thinking is community thinking. Individuals become healthy persons only in community with others. The people are not sovereign, and neither is the community. The community shapes the people and gives them freedom. The people shape the community and give it a measure of authority. Local communities are not sovereign. They can be healthy and strong only through their relation with other communities in a community of communities. That inclusive community is not sovereign. It exists to serve the communities that make it up, but these communities need for it to have its own measure of authority over them.

Substance thinking leads to the idea that if one institution increases in power, other institutions must lose power. Process thinking argues instead that no one can have any significant power except through cooperation. Increasing the power of the agencies of cooperation increases the power of those who cooperate through them. The most important form of power is that which empowers others. A world in which that is deeply understood can be a sustainable world.

CHAPTER FIVE

WINDS OF THE SPIRIT: THE SPIRITUAL FOUNDATIONS OF AN ECOLOGICAL CIVILIZATION

Humans cannot live by good ideas and public policies alone. Nor can they live by concern about the world's problems alone or by anger over the world's injustices. Frederic Buechner observed that our calling is that place where the gladness of our hearts meets the hungers of the world. If we are to help heal a broken world in whatever ways are possible for us, we must find a place of gladness. In this book we call it spirituality.

We begin this page with a quotation from a theologian, John Caputo. He writes:

> Be like the lilies, without why and without care. They bend and blow under the gentle listing of the breeze, which is the ruach Elohim, the soft winds of the spirit blowing across the epochs from creation that caress us.

With Caputo let's say that there are soft winds of the spirit blowing across the epochs from creation and that we can be caressed by them in our daily lives. The winds are not all-controlling or all-powerful. They can be overwhelmed by storms of our own making: wars, injustices, cruelties inflicted upon other people and animals, cruelties inflicted on ourselves. But the winds are good, gentle and refreshing, and they never give up on us. Even after storms the soft winds return with their grace, keeping life in motion. They are the winds of kindness and beauty, justice and joy, intimacy and merrymaking.

These winds cannot be locked within a box or placed within a verbal frame. They cannot be contained in a specific creed or ritual, or owned by a single community of believers. They are open and free. Spirituality is attunement to these winds so that we become their carriers in daily life. The winds need not be named in order to be carried. They can be understood naturalistically, theistically, or in both ways. The interpretation is less important than the attunement.

Understood in this way spirituality is everywhere. You find it in people who are spiritually interested but not religiously affiliated: that is, in spiritually independents. You find it in people who are primarily secular or naturalistic in their outlook, not interested in talk of "higher powers" and "deeper sources." And you find it in people who belong to a religious community and follow a religious path, including people who believe in a personal God who loves the world. The winds of the spirit are free and can be felt and known by all.

In moments when we are attuned to these winds, we feel more alive and awake, more fully ourselves. Often, however, we find ourselves spiritually stagnant. This may be especially true in a civilization that turns everything into objects for human use, and that measures all achievements in terms of fame, fortune, and power. We lose track of the winds and lose touch with ourselves.

Spiritual renewal is needed. Ecological Civilization is about spiritual integration: that is, an integration of the various aspects of a person's life so that he or she discovers and lives from a gladness of the heart.

What is this gladness? It is not happiness alone; indeed, it can flourish in sad and hard times. For us, one of the best sources for understanding it is the spiritual alphabet developed by Frederic and Mary Ann Brussat of Spirituality and Practice. They help us name the many forms of gladness — of inner aliveness — that are available to people all over the world: attention, beauty, being present, compassion, connections, devotion, enthusiasm, faith, forgiveness, grace, gratitude, hope, hospitality, imagination, hope, hospitality, imagination, joy, justice, kindness, listening, love, meaning, mystery, nurturing, openness, peace, play, questing, reverence, shadow (owning our suffering and sin), silence, teachers (learning from), transformation, unity, vision, wonder, x – a sense of mystery, yearning, you (positive self-regard), and zeal (zest for life).

We think of these as qualities of heart and mind, forms of relatedness that are part of the fullness of life. In the language of positive psychology, they are forms of emotional intelligence and embodied wisdom. In the language of theology, they are ways of being attuned to the winds of the spirit blowing across the epochs of creation. They are necessary for helping build compassionate communities and they are at the same time the fruit of such communities.

For some people in some situations, the primary aim of becoming more fully alive is individual happiness, albeit in community with others. Very old people and very young people are often in this situation, as are people who suffer from various kinds of illnesses. Individual happiness, even if only in fleeting moments of joy, is a good in its own right.

But for many people the activity of becoming more fully alive is connected with serving the well-being of local communities and the broader world. Local communities enjoy "well-being" to the degree that they are creative, compassionate, participatory, inclusive, humane to animals, good for the earth, and spiritually satisfying – with no one left behind. Such communities, as we have said, are the building blocks of Ecological Civilization.

The kind of spirituality we recommend – with its many forms of emotional intelligence and embodied wisdom — need not be consciously practiced in order to be effective. Many people seek to grow in emotional intelligence and spiritual wisdom without being intentional about the growth and without calling it "spirituality." Some practitioners are religiously affiliated and some are not. Some are young and some are old. Some believe in a higher power, some do not, and many are somewhere in between. They form a network of spiritually-interested seekers who understand the world around them, and the universe as a whole, as a communion of subjects and not simply a collection of objects.

We close where we began, with a word about the source of the calling. We suggested that the source can be named and understood in different ways, and that it need not be named at all. We offered four words to name it: Life, God, Love, and Beauty. We close by briefly sharing more of our own understanding of the source as God.

GOD

As explained in the Introduction, we write this book as Christians, but we have not been speaking to Christians alone. Indeed, we suspect that many of our most sensitive readers will be people of other faiths and people without any religious affiliation. All of this is for the good. The world would be a sad place if there were one religion, one philosophy, one outlook on life that is required of all if they are to live with respect and care for the community of life. Our view is but one, and it is that of process theology, with its unique way of thinking about God.

In Christianity one common way is on the analogy of a male political ruler who presides over his subjects, issuing commands and threatening reward and judgment. The philosopher Alfred North Whitehead once observed that this involves rendering unto God that which belongs to Caesar. Sometimes this monarchical image of God is accompanied by images of war. The divine Caesar is envisioned as a holy warrior who fights evil with evil, enjoying the vengeance he reaps upon others. Those who fight in the name of this divine Caesar then imagine themselves as on His side, sharing in the vengeance. They feel happy — as if they have accomplished something for the world and for God — when others suffer.

Another way to think of God is intimated in the analogy of an encompassing and inclusive receptacle — filled with compassion — within which all living beings live and move and have their being. This way of thinking about God is sometimes called panentheism because it emphasizes that all things are "in" God, even as God is more than all things added together. It envisions God, not on the analogy of Caesar, but on the analogy of Christ's own spacious heart.

In this more panentheistic perspective, God is equally present to all things, just like the ocean is equally present to all fish in the sea. This means that there is nowhere where God is not "always already present." God is "always already present" in Iraq and the United States, in North Korea and in South Korea, in India and in Pakistan, and in many other parts of the world. God is everywhere at once, and never reducible to a being among beings in the sky.

Christians who advocate panentheism suggest further that God is present in human life in two ways: as an indwelling lure toward nonviolent love relative to the situation at hand and as a great compassion who "feels the feelings" of all living beings as those feelings occur, sharing in their joys and sufferings. Christians typically call the first way "the indwelling call of God's spirit" and the second way as "the empathy or compassion of God."

In times threatened by war, the panentheistic perspective can be especially helpful. It suggests that even God suffers from the violence of war, sharing in the suffering of people on both sides. And it suggests that God is within all people, all over the world, as an indwelling lure toward nonviolence, which is itself a Christ-like form of love.

Moreover, panentheism suggests that God needs the world for God's will to be accomplished. Just as fish in the ocean have some degree of freedom from the presence of the ocean, such that they can move in this way or that way, so panentheism suggests that human beings have some degree of freedom from God, such that they can act in this way or that. The calling of God within the human heart requires cooperation, on the part of human beings, for its very fulfillment. Without that cooperation there will be tragedy, even in God. This is how some Christians understand the cross of Christ. It reveals what has always been the case: that wherever there is suffering and sadness, that suffering and sadness is shared by God.

When humans cooperate with the indwelling lure of God, what does it look like? One of the great peacemakers of the last century — Mahatma Gandhi — called it "peace." Whatever words we use, one thing is clear. Today there is a deep desire for this kind of peace to emerge on our planet. All over the planet people want to live lightly on the earth and gently with each other, even as their leaders may sometimes wish otherwise. From the perspective of panentheism, their desire for peace and love is not simply human. It is also divine. It is the very life of God, within each human heart, praying that the will of God might be done on earth as it is in heaven. It is up to us — all of us — that this prayer be realized. We write this book as an act of hope and, like Deborah, an act of prayer. May life and its source of hope, however named and understood, hear from us.

TOPICAL LINE DRIVES

Straight to the Point in under 44 Pages

All Topical Line Drives volumes are priced at $5.99 print and $2.99 in all eb-ook formats.

Available

The Authorship of Hebrews: The Case for Paul	David Alan Black
What Protestants Need to Know about Roman Catholics	Robert LaRochelle
What Roman Catholics Need to Know about Protestants	Robert LaRochelle
Forgiveness: Finding Freedom from Your Past	Harvey Brown, Jr.
God the Creator: Toward a More Robust Doctrine of Creation	Henry Neufeld
Process Theology: Embracing Adventure with God	Bruce Epperly
Holistic Spirituality: Life Transforming Wisdom from the Letter of James	
	Bruce Epperly
To Date or Not to Date: What the Bible Says about Pre-Marital Relationships	
	D. Kevin Brown
The Eucharist: Encounters with Jesus at the Table	Robert D. Cornwall
The Authority of Scripture in a Postmodern Age: Some Help from Karl Barth	
	Robert D. Cornwall
Rendering unto Caesar	Chris Surber
The Caregiver's Beattitudes	Robert Martin
What is Wrong with Social Justice	Elgin Hushbeck, Jr.
I'm Right and You're Wrong	Steve Kindle
Words of Woe: Alternative Lectionary Texts	Robert D. Cornwall
Stewardship: God's Way of Recreating the World	Steve Kindle
Those Footnotes in Your New Testament	Thomas W. Hudgins
Jonah: When God Changes	Bruce G. Epperly
Ruth & Esther: Women of Agency and Adventure	Bruce G. Epperly
Faith in a Time of Pandemic	Bruce G. Epperly
Beauty and Process Theology (coming soon)	Patricia Adams Farmer

Generous Quantity Discounts Available
Dealer Inquiries Welcome
Energion Publications — P.O. Box 841
Gonzalez, FL 32560
Website: http://energionpubs.com
Phone: (850) 525-3916

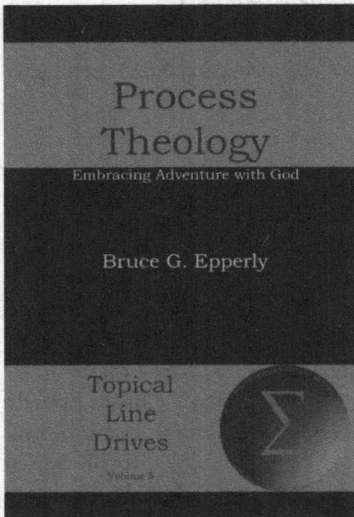

Process theology in less than
50 pages!

This one hits it out of the park.

David Alan Black
Dave Black Online
http://daveblackonline.com/blog.htm

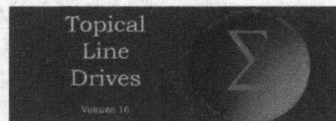

www.ingramcontent.com/pod-product-compliance
Lightning Source LLC
Chambersburg PA
CBHW010039040426
42331CB00037B/3326